The Power of a Subconscious Mind

Introduction

I've seen miracles happen to men and women in all walks of life worldwide. This book is meant to teach you to form, fashion, and create your destiny with your natural thinking and imagery, for as a man thinks in his subconscious mind, so is he. Do you know the answers?

Why is one man sad and another happy? Why is one man happy, prosperous, and another sad, miserable? Why is one man terrified and anxious, and another full of trust? Why is there a lovely, spacious home for one man, while another man lives a slum-life? Why is one guy tremendous and another an abject failure? Why is one speaker an excellent and hugely famous career, while the other man works and travels his entire life without creating or accomplishing anything worthwhile? Why is one man cured of so-called incurable illness, not another? Why are so many goods, kind religious people enduring damned torment in their minds and bodies? Why do so unethical and unfaithful people flourish and enjoy radiant health? Why are one woman happily married and her sister angry, unhappy? Are there answers to these questions? There's certainly.

You have a secret strength, such a remarkable skill that your life can be changed until you learn to use your life properly. This power is your subconscious mind. Many people tend to underestimate the power of their subconscious mind because they do not know what the subconscious mind is like or how it operates. You may also have assumed that the subconscious mind is an odd or mysterious or even a tabuous phenomenon. The unconscious mind is, however, a normal and essential part of your way of functioning.

However, make no mistake; the subconscious mind is still safe. I call it a hidden force so many people don't know how to use it. But I will show you how I can change your life with this hidden force in this book. Your subconscious mind will assist you in achieving goals, removing bad habits and replacing them with good ones, improving your self-identity, being a faster student and much more. You will experience more pleasure and happiness, more success, more financial wealth, better health and stronger relationships than you ever believed possible if you learn how to harness the power of your unconscious mind correctly. We will speak to you about what the subconscious mind is, how it functions, and how to reprogram it to make the life you are looking for your partner.

But let me explain something important that often confuses people before we start. Note always that when we talk about the conscious mind and the unconscious mind you have a single mind. But your one cause has two distinctive features, so that psychologists have called the conscious mind and the unconscious mind.

However, make no mistake; the subconscious mind is still safe. I call it a hidden force so many people don't know how to use it. But I will show you how I can change your life with this hidden force in this book. Your subconscious mind will assist you in achieving goals, removing bad habits and replacing them with good ones, improving your self-identity, being a faster student and much more. You will experience more pleasure and happiness, more success, more financial wealth, better health and stronger relationships than you ever believed possible if you learn how to harness the power of your unconscious mind correctly. We will speak to you about what the subconscious mind is, how it functions, and how to reprogram it to make the life you are looking for your partner.

But let me explain something important that often confuses people before we start. Note always that when we talk about the conscious mind and the unconscious mind you have a single mind. But your one cause has two distinctive features, so that psychologists have called the conscious mind and the unconscious mind.

Chapter 1: The Treasure House Inside You

You have a hidden power within you, ability so remarkable that it can transform your life once you learn how to use it properly. Your subconscious mind is that power. Many individuals appear to underestimate their subconscious mind's influence because they don't know what the subconscious mind is or how it functions. You might also have been led to believe that the subconscious mind is an unusual or enigmatic phenomenon or even a taboo. However, the subconscious mind is a natural and integral component of the way your mind operates.

Nevertheless, please make no mistake about it; the subconscious mind is healthy indeed. As most people don't know how to use it, I call it a hidden power. But in this book, I'm going to show you how to change your life by using this secret force. Your subconscious mind will help you accomplish goals, remove bad habits, and replace them with good ones, boost your self-image, be more innovative, become a faster learner, and so much more. When you learn how to harness the power of your subconscious mind correctly, you will experience more happiness and joy, more prosperity, more financial abundance, better health, and stronger relationships than you ever thought possible. We'll discuss what the subconscious mind is in this book, how it works, and how to work with it to reprogram it to be your partner in creating the life you want.

But let me give an essential clarification on something that sometimes confuses people before we begin. Always remember that you have ONE mind while we speak about the conscious mind and the subconscious mind. Yet your one reason has two distinct characteristics that are so distinctive that psychologists have given those two names the conscious mind and the subconscious mind.

1.1 The Tremendous Force of The Subconscious of Yours

By learning to touch and release the secret force of your subconscious mind, you will bring into your life more power, more money, more health, more happiness, and more joy.

You can gain the knowledge and understanding necessary to follow the simple techniques and processes in this book. A new light can empower you, and a new force can be created that helps you realize your hopes and make all your dreams come true. Decide now to make your life better, better, wealthier, and nobler than ever. There is infinite wisdom, infinite power, and endless supply within your subconscious depths of all that is needed, waiting for development and expression. Start now to grasp these potentialities of your deeper mind, and they will take shape without them in the world.

In every moment of time and point of space, the infinite intelligence within your subconscious mind can reveal to you everything you need to know, provided you are open-minded and receptive. You can get new ideas and thoughts that allow you to produce new inventions, make discoveries, or write books and plays. Besides, the infinite wisdom in your sub-conscious will impart excellent kinds of original-nature knowledge to you. It will reveal you and open the way to your life's perfect expression and the right location. You will attract the ideal friend and the right business associate or partner through the experience of your subconscious mind. It will find the right home buyer and give you all the money you need, as well as the financial freedom to be, to do, and to go, as your heart wishes.

You can discover your secret light, love, and beauty, of thought, feeling, and power. Though intangible, its capabilities are mighty. There is a solution to a problem within your subconscious mind and the cause for every effect. You come into real possession of the power and wisdom necessary to move forward in abundance, security, joy, and dominion because you can draw out the hidden forces.

I have seen the force of the subconscious lift people from crippled nations, once again making them whole, vital, and healthy, and free to go out into the world to enjoy happiness, fitness, and joyful speech. There is a miraculous healing force that can restore your troubled mind and a broken heart in your subconscious. It is capable of opening the prison door of the mind and freeing you. It will liberate you from material and physical slavery of all kinds.

1.2 The Need for A Working Basis

In the absence of a working basis that is universal in its implementation, significant advancement in any area of endeavor is unlikely. You may become an expert in the function of your subconscious mind. With a certainty of outcomes, you can exercise its forces in exact proportion to your interpretation of its values and your application of them for particular specific purposes and objectives that you want to accomplish. Being a chemist, I would like to point out that if you combine the proportions of two atoms of hydrogen and oxygen from the former to one of the latter, the result would be water. You are very familiar that carbon monoxide, a poisonous gas, can contain one atom of oxygen and one atom of carbon. But, if you add another oxygen atom, you're going to get carbon dioxide, an innocuous gas, and so on, all over the vast realm of chemical compounds. You do not accept that chemistry, physics, and mathematics' laws vary from your subconscious mind's rules. Let us take a widely accepted principle into account: "Water finds its level." This is principle applies everywhere to water.

Consider a different principle: "When heated, matter expands."

In all circumstances, this is valid. If we Heat a steel piece, it will expand in China, England, or India, regardless of whether the steel is found. It's a universal truth that when hot, matter expands. It is l truth that whatever you impress upon your subconscious mind is conveyed as a situation, experience, and event on the screen of space.

Your prayer is answered because the principle is your subconscious mind, and I mean the way a thing functions by principle. The focus of electricity, for instance, is that it operates from a higher to a lower potential. When you use it, you do not alter the concept of energy. Still, by cooperating with nature, you will bring forth beautiful inventions and discoveries that bless humanity in countless ways.

Your subconscious mind is the theory and acts under the rule of faith. You need to know what faith is, why it works, and how it functions. In a direct, straightforward, and beautiful way, your Bible says:

Whosoever shall say to this mountain, Thou shalt be moved again, and thou shalt be thrown into the sea; and he shall not doubt in his heart, but shall believe that the things which he saith shall come to pass; whatsoever he saith, that shall he have. 11:23 MARK.

Your mind's law is the law of belief. It implies believing in the way your mind works, considering in faith itself. Your mind's idea is your mind's thinking, which is simple, just that and nothing else.

Your subconscious mind's responses to your thoughts are all your perceptions, events, situations, and acts. Know, it is not the thing you believe in, but the conviction that contributes to the outcome in your head. Avoid believing in humanity's false views, opinions, superstitions, and fears. Start to believe in life's eternal truths and truths, which never change. You will step forward, then, and upward, and Godward.

Whoever reads this book and applies the concepts of the subconscious mind herein will pray for him and others scientifically and effectively. According to the law of action and reaction, your prayer is answered. Incipient motion is thought. The answer is the reaction of your subconscious mind that corresponds to the essence of your thinking. In your life, occupy your mind with the concepts of harmony, health, peace, and goodwill, and wonders will occur

1.3 The Mind Duality

You have only one mind, but two distinctive characteristics are present in your mind. Both thinking men and women today are well acquainted with the line of demarcation between the two. The two functions of your mind are, in essence, different. Everyone is endowed with distinct and separate attributes and forces. In order to differentiate the two parts of your mind, the nomenclature is usually used as follows: the objective and subjective reason, the conscious and subconscious mind, the waking and sleeping mind, the surface self and the deep self, the voluntary and involuntary mind, the male and the female, and several other words. Throughout this book, you will see the comments "conscious" and "subconscious" used to describe the dual nature of your mind.

1.4 The Minds That Are Conscious and Subconscious

Looking at your mind as a garden is an excellent way to get familiar with your mind's two functions. You are a gardener, and all day long, based on your habitual thinking, you plant seeds (thoughts) in your subconscious mind. When you grow in your subconscious mind, so is your body and environment, can you reap?

Start sowing thoughts of peace, joy, right action, goodwill, and prosperity now. Think about these qualities quietly and with interest and accept them entirely in your conscious reasoning mind. Continue to plant in your mind's garden these excellent seeds (thoughts), and you will reap a glorious harvest. Your subconscious mind is like soil that grows all sorts of sources, good or bad. Are men gathering grapes with thorns, or figs with thistles? Therefore, every thought is a cause, and every situation is an effect. For this reason, to bring forth only desirable conditions, you must take charge of your thoughts.

When your mind thinks appropriately, when you understand reality, when positive, harmonious, and happy are the thoughts stored in your subconscious mind, your subconscious magic working power will react and bring about agreeable circumstances, friendly surroundings, and the best of all. You will apply your subconscious forces to any issue or problem as you begin to manage your thought processes. In other words, you are merely going to cooperate knowingly with the infinite power and omnipotent law that governs all. Look around you wherever you live. You will notice that in the world without, the vast majority of humanity lives, the more enlightened people are intensely interested in the world within. Remember, it is the world within you that makes your world without your thoughts, feelings, and imagery.

Therefore, it is the only creative power, and everything you find in your world of expression has been created consciously or unconsciously by you in the inner world of your mind. Awareness of your conscious and subconscious minds' relationship will help you to change your entire life. It would be best if you altered the cause to change external conditions. Many men attempt to improve situations and circumstances by coping with circumstances and needs. You must remove the cause to eliminate discord, confusion, lack, limitation, and the reason events use a severe mind. In other words, the way you think in your head and imagine it. In a fathomless sea of infinite riches, you live. Your subconscious is very susceptible to your ideas. Of course, from a mental, emotional, and material point of view, there can be no more beautiful blessings than these. Most great scientists, artists, poets, singers, writers, and inventors have deeply understood the workings' conscious and subconscious minds.

One time, the great operatic tenor, Caruso, was struck by stage fright. His throat was paralyzed because of spasms caused by intense fear, which restricted his throat muscles, he said. Perspiration copiously poured down his face. He was ashamed because he had to go out on stage in a couple of minutes, yet he was shaking with fear and trepidation. He said, 'They're going to laugh at me. "I can't sing." Then he screamed, "The Little Me wants to strangle the Big Me inside" in the presence of those behind the stage.

"He told the Little Me," Get out of here, and the Big Me wants to sing through me. "He meant the infinite strength and intelligence of his subconscious mind by the Big Me, and he started yelling," Get out, get out, the Big Me is going to sing! His subconscious mind responded, releasing within him the vital forces.

He walked off the stage when the call came and sang gloriously and majestically, captivating the audience.

It is clear to you that Caruso must have understood the two levels of mind, the subconscious or irrational level, and the conscious or rational level. Your subconscious mind is receptive to the essence of your thoughts and reacts. The negative emotions generated in your subconscious mind (the Big Me) are released and flood the conscious mind with a sense of panic, foreboding, and despair when your conscious mind (the little me) is full of fear, worry, and anxiety. When such things happen, you can talk to the irrational emotions produced in your deeper mind, like Caruso, affirmatively and with a deep sense of authority, as follows: "Be still, be quiet, I am in charge, you must obey me, you are subject to my command, you cannot intervene everywhere."

It is intensely interesting to observe how you can speak to the irrational movement of your more profound self-bringing silence, harmony, and peace in your mind with authority and conviction. The subconscious is direct to the conscious mind, which is why it is called subconscious or subjective.

1.5 Outstanding Differences and Operation Modes

You can interpret the key differences with the following examples: The conscious mind is like a navigator or a captain on a ship's bridge. He directs the ship to the men in the engine room and signals orders, who control all the boilers, instruments, gauges, etc. The men in the engine room are unaware of where they are going; they are following orders. If the man on the bridge follows wrong instructions based on his results with the compass, sextant, or other tools, they will go on the rocks. The engine room men follow him because he is in charge and gives instructions immediately obeyed. Members of the crew do not talk back to the captain; they carry out orders.

The master of his ship is the captain, and his decrees are carried out. Likewise, the captain and the master of your craft, which represents your body, atmosphere, and all your affairs, is your conscious minded on what your conscious mind believes and accepts as correct, your subconscious mind takes the orders you give it. When you repeatedly say to people, "I can't afford it," then your subconscious mind takes you at your word and sees to it that you will not be in a position to buy what you want. As long as you continue to say, "I can't afford that car, that trip to Europe, that house, that coat of fur or wrap of ermine," you can rest assured that your subconscious mind will obey your instructions, and you will go through life feeling the absence of all these things.

A stunning young university student looked at an enticing and very costly travel bag in a shop window last Christmas Eve. She was going home to Buffalo, New York, for the holidays. When she recalled something, she had heard at one of my lectures, she was about to say, "I can't afford that bag," which was, "Never finish a negative statement; reverse it immediately, and wonders will happen in your life."

"She said," Mine is that bag. It is for purchase. I emotionally embrace it, and my subconscious sees that I am getting it.

Her fiancé presented her with a bag the same as the one she had looked at eight o'clock on Christmas Eve and mentally remembered herself at ten o'clock the same morning. She filled her mind with the thought of hope and released the whole thing to her more profound sense, which has the "know-how" of achievement. At the University of Southern California, this young lady, a student at the University of Southern California, said to me, "I didn't have the money to buy that bag, but now I know where to find money and all the stuff I need, and what's inside me in the treasure house of eternity." Another easy example is this: when you say, "I don't like mushrooms," and then you get the chance to have mushrooms served in sauces or sauces. "Her subconscious mind nudges her whenever she drinks coffee as if to suggest, "The boss needs you to stay awake tonight." Your subconscious mind works twenty-four hours a day and makes arrangements for your benefit, pouring into your lap all the fruit of your everyday thinking. A woman might say, "When I drink coffee at night, I wake up at three o'clock."

1.6 The Way Subconscious Reacted

A woman wrote to me: "I am seventy-five years old, a widow with a grown family." I lived on my own and a pension. I heard your lectures on the subconscious mind's forces, where you said that through repetition, trust, and hope, ideas could be transmitted to the subconscious mind. "I often started to repeat, feeling, 'I'm wanted. I am married to a man of kindness, love, and a spiritual mind. I'm sure! For around two weeks, I kept doing this several times a day, and I was introduced to a retired pharmacist one day at the corner drug store.

I discovered that he was kind, understanding, and very religious. The response to my prayer was a beautiful one.

He proposed to me within a week, and now we're on our honeymoon in Europe. I know that in my subconscious mind, wisdom brought us both together in divine order. This woman discovered that there was a treasure house inside.

Her prayer was felt to be real in her heart, and her affirmation sank into her subconscious mind, which is the creative medium, through osmosis. The moment she managed to bring about a subjective embodiment, her subconscious mind brought about the answer through the law of attraction. Full of wisdom and knowledge, her more profound sense took both of them together in the divine order.

Be sure that you think about whatever stuff is real, whatever stuff is truthful, whatever stuff is, whatever stuff is pure, whatever stuff is lovely, whatever stuff is good to report; if there is any virtue, and any praise, think about these things.

1.7 How to Think Richly

It's accepting something to believe as correct. There is an absolute difference between wealth and poverty, health and sickness, achievement, and failure is made by belief. Believe in, and you can sense the Infinite Force's wealth inside your subconscious. When your issues seem overwhelming, break the tension by praying tirelessly for someone who is sick or in deep distress, and you will instantly find your problems solved. Ensure the ailment or any part of the body is not identified when praying for a loved one. Realize that the Divine Presence of Redemption flows through the precious one as peace, health, goodwill, and joy. Visualize as radiant and cheerful the person you love. Meditate gently on these truths and pray once again when you are expected to do so. Miracles arise when you pray this way. Sympathy means going down and not helping the sick to the twists, and with each other.

Have compassion and give the suffering person a transfusion of faith, trust, and devotion, knowing that with God, all things are possible. Your mind is imaginative, and it seems like any idea makes itself manifest. You can direct and push your thoughts in the same way that you steer your car. Your thought-image of wealth, success, and accomplishment is the magnet that attracts all things to you that correspond with your thought-image. The calm mind gets the right things done. When your conscious mind is still, and your body is relaxed, your subconscious experience will arrive at the surface mind. A good executive knows how authority can be delegated. You must be a good executive by using your mind. Turn your request to your subconscious with trust and faith, and you will get the right answer. When you finally turn it over, you know, because you're at peace with yourself.

You will give up smoking or another terrible habit by decreeing liberty and peace of mind while simultaneously imagining a friend or a doctor congratulating you on your room. When you affirm and image an antipathy towards tobacco, your subconscious will take over and push your emancipation from the trend. Many have discovered the wisdom of turning God-Presence over to an urgent domestic crisis, believing that Divine wisdom and knowledge would bring about the best solution for all. Many have discovered the understanding of turning God-Presence over to an urgent domestic crisis, believing that Divine wisdom and knowledge would bring about the best solution for all. Liquidate the past and never hold on to grudges or old concerns. Your current thinking, which has been made manifest, is the future. Think often and systematically of peace, beauty, loyalty, goodwill, and abundance, and you will have a great lot. Our children don't own us. When issues emerge with an infant, pray as follows: Whenever you think of your child, praise him or her secretly by knowing, "God loves my child and cares about my child." It will be safe when you do this, whatever happens.

A dream of boundless wealth inside your subconscious mind. Think about peace, satisfaction, happiness, compassion, guidance, right action, progress. All these are the ideals of life, and when you think of life more abundantly, you release the latent powers within you. Your subconscious will force you to express an abundant life right here and right now. To assure yourself of the incredible power of faith, use meditation.

Chapter 2: How Your Mind Works

You've got a mind, and you need to learn how to use it. The conscious or logical level and the subconscious or irrational level is two layers of your mind. Through your conscious mind, you think, and whatever you believe, usually sinks into your subconscious mind, which, according to the nature of your thoughts, produces. Your subconscious mind is the brick of your thoughts and is the mind of creation. Goodwill follows if you think well; if you feel bad, bad will follow. This is the mind's way of functioning.

If the subconscious mind embraces an idea, the primary point to note is to execute it. That the rule of the subconscious mind functions for both good and bad ideas is a fascinating and subtle reality; this rule is the source of failure, anger, and unhappiness when applied negatively. However, you achieve perfect fitness, success, and prosperity when your everyday thinking is harmonious and positive.

When you start thinking and feeling in the right way, peace of mind and a safe body are inevitable. Your subconscious mind will embrace and bring forth into your reality anything you say mentally and believe as real. The only thing you need to do is get your subconscious mind to embrace your idea, and the rule of your subconscious mind will bring about your desired health, harmony, or place. You send the order or decree, and the concept impressed upon it is diligently reproduced by your subconscious desires. The rule of your mind is this: According to the essence of the thought or idea you keep in your conscious mind, you will get a reaction or response from your subconscious mind. Psychologists and psychologists find out that impressions are created in the brain cells as emotions are communicated through the subconscious mind. As soon as your subconscious embraces some definition, it immediately continues to bring it into effect. It works by integrating ideas and using every bit of experience you have gained to accomplish its function in your lifetime. It draws on the power, energy, and wisdom that is infinite within you. To get its way, it lines up all of the rules of nature. It appears to bring about an immediate solution to your problems sometimes, but it can take days, weeks, or longer at other times. His ways have been discovered.

2.1 Differentiated by Conscious And Subconscious Words

You should keep it in mind that these are not two minds. Within one mind, they are merely two spheres of operation. The reasoning mind is your conscious mind. It is the process of the mind that determines. For instance, in life, you choose your books, your home, and your partner. With a conscious mind, you make all your choices.

On the other hand, your heart is kept automatically functioning without any deliberate decision on your part, and your subconscious mind carries on the mechanism of digestion, circulation, and breathing through processes outside of your conscious control. Your subconscious mind embraces what is impressed with it or what you believe consciously. Like your conscious mind, it does not reason things out, and it does not disagree controversially with you. Your subconscious mind is like the ground that embraces every seed, good or bad, of any sort. Your thoughts are alive, and they can be compared to seeds. In your subconscious mind, negative, harmful thoughts begin to function negatively and will come into an outer experience that coincides with them in due time.

Know, your subconscious mind does not participate in proving whether your thoughts are good or bad, real or false, but it responds to your thoughts or suggestions according to their existence. For instance, even if it may be false, if you actively believe anything as true, your subconscious mind will accept it as true and continue to produce results, which would inevitably follow, since you have actively assumed it to be true.

2.2 The Immense Power of Suggestion

By now, you must know that the "Watchman at the gate" is your conscious mind, and its chief purpose is to shield your subconscious mind from false perceptions. You are now conscious of one of the universal laws of the mind:

Your subconscious mind is ideal for a recommendation. As you know, your subconscious mind doesn't allow contrasts or similarities, nor does it reason and figure things out for itself. Your conscious mind belongs to this latter role. It responds simply to your conscious mind's impressions given to it. It does not indicate a preference over another for one course of action. A classic instance of the immense influence of suggestion is the following. Suppose you approach a shy-looking passenger on board a ship and say something like this to him: "You look very sick." How pale are you! I feel sure you're going to be seasick. "Let me go to your cabin to help you." The passenger turns pale. His worries and predictions are correlated with your suggestion of seasickness. He brings your assistance down to the berth, and your negative advice, which he embraced, is realized there.

2.3 Various Responses to The Same Suggestion

It is true that, because of their subconscious conditioning or conviction, various individuals can respond to the same suggestion in different ways. "For instance, if you go to a sailor on a ship and say sympathetically to him," My dear fellow, you look very sick. You don't feel sick? "You always stare at me as if you are going to be seasick." He either laughs at your "joke," according to his disposition or shows a slight annoyance. In this case, your suggestion fell on deaf ears because your suggestion of seasickness was synonymous with his immunity from it in his view. It did not, however, call for fear or worry, but self-confidence.

The dictionary notes that a suggestion is an act or example of placing something in one's mind, the mental process by which the suggested thought or concept is entertained, embraced, or enforced. You must note that, against the conscious mind's will, a suggestion cannot force anything on the subconscious mind. Your conscious mind, in other words, has the power to reject the suggestion given. In sailor's situation, he was not afraid of seasickness. He had persuaded himself of his immunity, and there was simply no power for a negative suggestion to elicit fear. His indwelling fear of seasickness called out the idea of seasickness to the other passenger. We have his or her inner fears, values, thoughts, and lives controlled and controlled by these inner assumptions. A suggestion, even if you psychologically consider it, has no power in and of itself. This allows the subconscious powers to flow according to the suggestion's essence in a limited and restricted manner.

2.4 Developing Confidence and Self-Worth

There may be numerous explanations why one person in his or her profession or company is successful, and another is not. I have found that the most important ingredient that predestines a person to success or lack of success is how one feels about oneself over the many years that I have interacted with rich and poor, famous and ordinary people, leaders and followers. Those who genuinely love themselves, who believe that they are people of worth are much more likely than those who lack this confidence to achieve success in their lives. What is it that effective individuals possess that others do not? It is self-esteem or trust in oneself. They trust in themselves and the forces that are inside them. It is best to describe self-esteem as feeling good about oneself. People with high self-esteem think that most things they do are more likely to succeed. They love themselves and feel other individuals value them. This doesn't mean that they're always confident and are always happy and smiling about everything. We all have bad days and have moments where it all appears to be going wrong. This can be embraced by people with high self-esteem and not let it overpower them.

An integral part of self-confidence is self-esteem. It would help you if you trusted in yourself before you can feel confident about your choices. You have to feel like you're someone of importance. How would you be sure that your choices are worthwhile if you do not have self-esteem?

Why is self-confidence low in people? One common explanation is that early in their lives, they may have failed in some operation and fear this will happen again. Another is that other individuals have never pleased teachers or even their parents with their success in school or other matters and left them with a sense of inferiority.

Others still have tasted success only to have it accompanied by some disappointment and have caused their minds to be consumed by the disappointment and condemn them to a lack of self-confidence in everything they do. In your subconscious mind, the secret to changing your feelings about yourself resides. Through your conscious mind, the only way for you to enter your subconscious mind is. The dominant principle still governs your subconscious. Your subconscious would embrace the stronger of the two conflicting propositions. If you say, "I want self-confidence, but one can't get it; 1 try so hard; 1 force myself to pray; 1 use all the willpower 1 has," you need to recognize that your effort is focused on your mistake. Consider yourself never a disappointment.

You are governed by your calculations, your blueprints, and your opinions about yourself. It is not the opinion of any other person about you. What do you do if anyone says to you, "You're a failure; you'll never make up for anything"? Say to yourself, "It's meaningless what another person thinks about me. I'm born to win, to succeed. I must succeed. Spectacularly and especially, I'm going to succeed."

Every time anyone says you're going to fail, it's an incentive for you to reinforce your belief in your subconscious mind's power, which never fails. In other words, don't blame the shortcomings of others. Don't blame the terms. In order to overcome poor circumstances, effective people work. There'll be failures, of course, but that doesn't mean you're a failure. You have the imaginative strength within you to reverse failure, to move on to success. The other person does not control you. The ability to control you is not in the other person unless you authorize it. With each success you have, self-esteem increases inside you. When you encounter occasional failure, self-esteem will even grow if you remember that the power is still with you, and you believe it and have proven it by your actions.

You are what you believe yourself to be. In the picture you have of yourself in your head, you build yourself. Self-esteem and self-confidence are nothing more than your picture of yourself being projected. You would be a happier and more successful person if you maintain a good positive self-image. No matter how demanding and achieving the objectives you set for yourself, you will be an individual able to hurdle over roadblocks. Belief in yourself, what you are doing, and your ultimate destiny is your greatest need. When followed by a conviction that the real self is God-given and that with God, all things are possible, self-reliance or self-confidence or self-confidence seeks its greatest outlet.

Make your mind up, this minute, now. You may have what you want to own, and, as you believe, it will be done to you. Follow the age-old maxim: make sure that you are right and then go ahead. Let nothing move or shake the determination from you. Make it a component of your mindset. And you'll eventually excel and step on in life with this sort of confidence.

2.5 Meet Challenges and Beat Them

Self-confidence, when faced with losses, can be shaken. Plans go wrong, unforeseen hurdles emerge, and everything appears to crumble. The time to restore your faith in yourself is now. Now is the time to call all the reserves that God has given you and face the problem and conquer it. You will succeed, and you will improve your self-esteem in that performance. The best managers generally accept that the greater the barrier, the more self-confidence is needed, and the more influential the experience is in his early career, A. During the big Japanese earthquake and the Asian economic crisis, G. Lafley, who became the CEO of Procter & Gamble, was responsible for the Asian operations. He said that by never losing confidence in himself and bearing in mind that one learns ten times more in a crisis than regular times, he managed to lead his company through these formidable obstacles.

Similarly, in a crisis, Jeff Immelt, now CEO of General Electric (GE), was placed on the spot. CEO Jack Welch put him in charge of fixing the situation in 1 98 8 when millions of refrigerator compressors were defective, even though Immelt had no previous experience with refrigerators or recalls. He said that if he had not had faith in his ability to deal with that "impossible" task, a circumstance many in GE saw as an insurmountable challenge, there is no way he would be CEO today. Another example of a significant challenge being solved is that of CEO John Chambers at Cisco. As one of the most charismatic, electrifying speakers in the entire business world, he is well recognized. To make it appear off-the-cuff, he memorizes just enough of his presentation. To address individuals directly, he leaves the podium. Through his audience, he never loses eye contact. He is an onstage genius whose talks are characterized as "amazing" by the tough business press. It isn't easy to imagine that this articulate man had to conquer considerable challenges in order to give him the self-confidence to get up before an audience. And what gave him this self-confidence? The power he learned from having to overcome dyslexia. Chambers had to the device to speak to audiences at all in order to manage.

2.6 The Strength of An Assumed Significant Premise

Like a syllogism, the mind works. This implies that any big assumption your conscious mind believes to be valid defines the inference that your subconscious mind draws with respect to some specific question or issue in your mind. If your assumption is true, as, in the following example, the inference must be true: every virtue is laudable; friendliness is a virtue. Therefore, kindness is commendable. Another instance is as follows: All created things alter and pass away; Egypt's Pyramids are created things; thus, the Pyramids will pass away someday. The first argument is referred to as the principal assumption, and the correct conclusion must inevitably obey the correct assumption. A college professor at Town Hall, New York, who attended some of my Science of Mind lectures in May 1962, told me, "It's all topsy-turvy in my life, and I've lost health, money, and friends." Everything I touch turns out to be false.'

I explained to him that in his thought, he should create a significant premise that his subconscious mind's infinite intelligence directed, guided, and prospered him spiritually, mentally, and materially. Then, in his finances, decisions, and repairing his body and returning his mind to peace and quiet, his subconscious mind would naturally guide him. This professor conceived an overall idea of the way he wanted his life to be, and this was his key premise: "Infinite wisdom leads and directs me in all my ways." Perfect health is mine, and in my mind and body, the Law of Harmony works. Mine are elegance, passion, harmony, and abundance. My entire life is governed by the concept of right action and divine order. I know that my core concept is focused on life's eternal truths, and I know, feel, and believe that my subconscious mind reacts to the essence of my conscious mind thinking. "He wrote me as follows:" I slowly, softly, and lovingly repeated the above statements many times a day knowing that they were sinking deep into my subconscious mind and that results would follow. I'm profoundly thankful for the interview you gave me, and I want to add that all of my life's departments are changing for the better. It's functioning!

2.7 How to Think

It's accepting something as a right to believe. Belief makes the difference between prosperity and poverty, health and disease, success, and failure. Believe in, and you will feel, the wealth of the Limitless Force inside your subconscious. Break the stress by praying intensely for someone who is sick or in deep trouble when your problems seem unbearable, and immediately you will find your issues solved. When praying for a loved one, make sure that the ailment or some aspect of the anatomy is not known. Realize that the Divine Healing Presence flows as harmony, wellbeing, goodwill, and joy through the beloved one. Visualize the person you love as radiant and happy. Meditate on these truths softly and pray once more when you were supposed to do so. When you pray this way, miracles occur. Sympathy means going down to the twists and with each other, and not to help sick.

Have compassion and offer a transfusion of faith, trust, and love to the suffering person, knowing that all things are possible with God. Your mind is imaginative, and every idea appears to make itself manifest. In this way that you steer your vehicle; you can guide and drive your thoughts. Thoughts are artifacts. The magnet that draws all things to you correlates with your thought-image of riches, prosperity, and achievement. The quiet mind gets stuff done. Tell your body to be still, and quiet your mind by thinking of your subconscious infinite wisdom, which knows the answer. Your subconscious knowledge will come up to the surface mind when your conscious mind is still, and your body is relaxed. A good executive understands how to delegate power. When using your mind, you must be a good executive. With confidence and trust, turn your request over to your subconscious, and you will get the right response. You know when you truly turn it over because you are at peace with yourself. By decreeing freedom and peace of mind, you will give up smoking or another lousy habit while simultaneously imagining a friend or a doctor congratulating you on your space. Your subconscious will take over and drive your liberation from the pattern when you affirm and picture an antipathy toward tobacco. Many have discovered the wisdom of turning God-Presence over to an urgent domestic crisis, believing that Divine wisdom and knowledge would bring about the best solution for all. The prayer, "I let go and let God take over," offers the perfect answer. Liquidate the past and never hold to old concerns or grudges. The future is your present thought that has been made manifest. Think of harmony, elegance, devotion, goodwill, and abundance frequently and systematically, and you will have a great future. We don't own our kids. Pray as follows when problems occur with a child:

 Whenever you think of your child, secretly bless him or her by knowing, "God loves my child and cares for my child." When you do this, whatever happens, is going to be healthy. Inside your subconscious mind, a dream of the limitless riches. Think of harmony, happiness, joy, compassion, guidance, right action, achievement. All these are life values, and you trigger the dormant forces within you as you think of life more abundantly. Your subconscious will force you, right here and right now, to express an abundant life. Thoughts are artifacts. Use meditation to assure yourself of the incredible power of faith.

Chapter 3: Your Subconscious Miracle-Working Strength

Your subconscious power is enormous. It inspires you, guides you, and reveals names, facts, and scenes from the memory storehouse to you. Your subconscious starts your heartbeat, regulates your blood supply, and manages your digestion, assimilation, and removal.

When you eat bread, your subconscious mind transmuted into tissue, muscle, bone, and blood. The wisest man who walks the earth is this process. Your subconscious mind governs all of your body's essential techniques and functions and knows the solution to all problems. Your subconscious mind never rests, never sleeps. On the job, it's Al-ways. By clearly stating to your subconscious before sleep that you want a sure particular thing accomplished, you can discover the miracle-working power of your subconscious. You will be pleased to find that powers will be unleashed inside you, leading to the desired outcome. Here, then, is a power and knowledge source that puts you in contact with omnipotence or the power that moves the earth, directs the planets in their direction and makes the sunshine.

The source of your ideals, aspirations, and altruist urges your subconscious mind. Shakespeare interpreted great truths concealed from the ordinary man of his day, in the subconscious mind. Undoubtedly, it was his sub-conscious mind's response that caused the Greek sculptor, Phidias, to portray marble and bronze in beauty, order, symmetry, and proportion. It allowed symphonies to be written by the Italian artist, Raphael, to paint Madonnas and Ludwig van Beethoven.

I lectured at Yoga Forest University, Rishikesh, India, in 1955, and I spoke with a visiting surgeon from Mumbai there. He's been telling me about Dr.

A Scotch surgeon, James Esdaille, served in Bengal before either or other modern anesthesia methods were discovered. Dr. Es-daille conducted about four hundred primary operations of all kids between 1843 and 1846, such as amputations, tumor removal, and cancerous growths, as well as eye, ear, and throat operations. Operations were performed solely under mental anesthesia. In Rishikesh, this Indian doctor told me that Dr. Esdaille's patients' postoperative mortality rate was meager, possibly two or three percent.

Patients felt no pain, and during the surgery, there were no deaths.

Dr. Esdaille proposed that no illness or septic disease can arise in all his patients' subconscious minds, who were in a hypnotic state.

Many researchers pointed out the bacterial roots of the disease and its causes due to unsterilized instruments, and virulent organisms must note that this was the case.

This Indian surgeon said that Dr. Esdaille's suggestions to his patients' subconscious minds were undoubtedly the reason for the low mortality rate and the general absence of infection, which was reduced to a minimum. In compliance with the essence of his suggestion, they replied.

It is fantastic to consider how a surgeon discovered the miraculous wonder-working abilities of the subconscious mind over a hundred and twenty years ago. When you sit and think of the metaphysical powers of your subconscious mind, does it not cause you to be seized with a sort of spiritual awe? Consider their extra-sensory perceptions, such as their capacity for clairvoyance and clairaudience, their freedom from time and space, their ability to liberate you from all pain and suffering, and their ability to respond to all problems, whatever they may be. All these shows to you that there are strength and wisdom that far transcends your intellect, causing you to wonder at the wonders of its distress. All these encounters allow you to rejoice and believe in your own subconscious mind's miracle-working powers. Your subconscious is Your Life Book.

Whatever thoughts, convictions, views, ideas, or dogmas you write, engrave, or impress on your subconscious mind, you shall experience them as the objective manifestation of situations, conditions, and events.

What you write on the inside, on the outside, you can feel. You have two sides to your life, tangible and unseen, objective and subjective, thought and manifestation. Your brain receives your thinking, which is your mind's conscious thought organ. If your conscious or objective mindfully embraces the idea, it is sent to the solar plexus, called your mind's brain, where it becomes flesh and manifests in your experience. Your subconscious does not argue, as previously outlined. It only functions for what you write on it. It acknowledges your verdict or your conscious mind's conclusions as final. That's why you always write about the Book of Life because your thoughts become your experiences. Ralph Waldo Emerson, the American essayist, wrote, "A man is what he feels all day" is expressed by his subconscious mind.

William James said that the power to move the world is in your subconscious mind. With limitless knowledge and boundless wisdom, the subconscious mind is one. The springs and the rule of life feed it. Therefore, you have to inspire her with the right suggestions and positive thoughts. There are so much chaos and misery in the world that people do not understand the interaction of their conscious and subconscious minds. Hermes' tomb was opened with great expectancy and a sense of wonder because people believed that the greatest secret of the ages was contained therein.

Whatever you feel as real, subjectively is expressed as conditions, experiences, and events. Motion and emotion must balance. As in heaven [your mind], so on earth [in your body and environment]. It is the great law of life. You will find throughout all nature the direction of action and reaction, rest, and motion. These two must be in equilibrium, and then there will be harmony and balance. You are here to let the concept of life flow rhythmically and harmoniously through you. The intake and the result should be equal. There has to be a feeling and language that is similar. It must be identical in impression and expression. All your anxieties are because of unfulfilled desires.

If you do not think positively, destructively, and viciously, these thoughts generate destructive emotions that must be expressed and find an outlet. These emotions describe as ulcers, heart trouble, tension, and anxieties of a negative nature. What do you think or feel about yourself right now? Every part of your being conveys the concept. The reflection of the idea you have of yourself is your vitality, body, financial status, friends, and social status. It is the real meaning of what is impressed in your subconscious mind and expressed in your life phases. Through the bleak thoughts we entertain, we harm ourselves. How much have you been wounded by getting angry, scared, jealous, or vengeful? The poisons that penetrate your subconscious mind are these. With these pessimistic attitudes, you were not born. Feed your subconscious mind, life-giving feelings, and all the destructive habits therein will be washed out. All of the past will be washed out and remembered no more while you continue to do this.

3.1 The Subconscious Cures the Skin Malignancy

The most compelling proof of the healing power of the subconscious mind will still be personal healing. I resolved the spite of the skin through prayer over forty years ago. The growth did not test by medical therapy, and it was getting increasingly worse. With a piece of in-depth psychological knowledge, a clergyman explained to me the inner meaning of the 139th Psalm wherein it says, in thy book, all my members were written, which fashioned in continuance when none of them were yet.

He clarified that my subconscious mind, which fashioned and shaped all my organs from an invisible cell, meant the term novel. He also pointed out that since my subconscious mind made my body, it could again recreate it and heal it according to the perfect pattern.

This clergyman showed me his watch and said, "This was a designer, and before the watch became an objective reality, the watchmaker had to have the idea first in mind, and if the watch was out of order, the watchmaker might repair it." My friend reminded me that the subconscious intellect that formed my body was like a watchmaker. It also knew exactly how to heal, restore, and direct all the vital functions and processes of my body, but I had to give it the perfect health idea. It would act as a catalyst, and healing would be the result. "I prayed as follows:" In my subconscious mind, the divine intellect created my body and all its organs. It knows how to heal me. His knowledge fashioned all my organs, tissues, muscles, and bones. Inside me, this divine healing presence is now changing every atom of my being, making me whole and perfect now. I thank you for the healing that I know is taking place now.

"The works of creative intelligence inside me are marvelous." I prayed aloud two or three times a day for about five minutes, repeating the essential prayer. My skin was whole and acceptable in about three months.

All I did was give my subconscious mind life-giving patterns of wholeness, elegance, and perfection, thus obliterating the negative images and thinking ways stuck in my subconscious mind that caused all my trouble. Nothing appears on your body even when the emotional counterpart is first in your mind, and as you change your mind by drenching it with incessant affirmatives, you change your body. It is the basis of all healing.

3.2 The Subconscious Governs All Body Functions

Whereas the conscious mind is the part of your mind that you are aware of, the subconscious mind is considered the reason you are unaware of it. The subconscious mind is in action 24 hours a day, and at the same time, it can perform an infinite number of functions. It's like a machine running in your mind's background, continuously monitoring your involuntary processes, thoughts, and behaviors. Whether you are wide awake or deep asleep, without the aid of your conscious mind, your subconscious mind is always at work, monitoring all of your body's essential functions. You don't have to worry intentionally about breathing, making your heart pound, digesting your food, blinking your eyes, and so on. If you are sleeping or alert, your subconscious mind does all of that for you around the clock. Your subconscious mind interacts continuously with every cell in your body, receives feedback from those cells, and gives them instructions. The subconscious mind also handles all of the routine tasks that you had to learn through a thorough process with your conscious mind.

A classic example is a challenge of learning to drive a vehicle. Think back to when you learned to drive a car for the first time. At first, you had to think about everything you did purposely. A couple of years ago, I recalled teaching my daughter to drive. I had to say stuff like, "Now we're going to take the next street to the right." I want you to pull your foot away from the gas. Turn on your right blinker now. Put your foot on the brake, start turning the steering wheel to the right, straighten up the steering wheel now, take the brake off your foot, and put it back on the gas. In other words, she had to think consciously and be instructed intentionally on every move to make. But once she went through the conscious learning process, her brain and neuro pathways were created. Her subconscious mind eventually took over, so she didn't consciously think about every movement or action. And today, she's an outstanding driver, and her subconscious mind completely controls much of her driving. Most of the things you have consciously learned to ride a bike, tie your shoes, swim, you name it, are the same process. These are all examples of things you had to learn how to do consciously, through a painstaking process, but the subconscious mind took over after you went through the conscious process, and now you can do certain things without thinking about them consciously. Your subconscious mind learned to do such things because you did them repetitively through your conscious mind. One of the programming keys of the subconscious mind is repetition. (Remember the value of "repetition," because later in the book, we'll come back to it.) Here are several other subconscious mind characteristics. The conscious mind is logical. Ok, the subconscious mind is the part of the reason that is "emotional." It is the source of our feelings, including love, hate, happiness, sorrow, resentment, envy, rage, and joy. Emotion is also one of the keys to reprogramming the subconscious mind, as is repetition. The conscious mind is the minimal memory of the conscious mind. But that's not the case for the subconscious mind. There is a nearly infinite memory in the subconscious mind. In reality, everything you have experienced in your life (from the moment you were born), including every sight you have ever seen, every sound you have ever heard, and every emotion you have ever experienced. In your subconscious mind, they are all processed. And that takes me to the subconscious mind's role that will be this book's main focus. You hold beliefs in the subconscious mind, including whether you see yourself as talented or untalented, successful or unsuccessful, deserving of love, or undeserving of love.

These deep-seated assumptions about yourself are the product of all the experiences in your life, including your childhood experiences. And this is important because, as adults, we often retain many negative self-concepts and values in our subconscious minds formed in our childhood years. Children are sometimes told cruel things, and these things are quickly implanted into a child's subconscious mind, and often stay there for life. Classmates, siblings, or even parents and teachers may speak of these cruel comments made to children. Such examples are here:

You are fat

You are ugly, ugly,

You're silly, dumb

You're not lazy,

You're never going to amount to anything,

There's nothing you can do right now.

These negative beliefs are easily programmed deeply into the child's subconscious mind when statements such as these are repeatedly said to a child and with emotion. The subconscious mind accepts these negative statements as facts. And it is not just childhood experiences that the subconscious mind can be negatively conditioned. Bad encounters with adults will do the same thing. And the impact on your life can be drastic, regardless of when the negative programming takes place.

Here's why the beliefs you hold deep in your subconscious mind about yourself have a tremendous effect on the reality you are experiencing in your life. If you hold negative thoughts about yourself at the subconscious level, you will tend to experience negative realities in your life. You will begin to experience positive realities in your life if you have complimentary views about yourself. It is because, ultimately, your reality will match the subconscious image you have of yourself. That statement let me repeat because it's such a crucial point. Your truth will eventually fit the subconscious picture you have of yourself.

Here's how it works. I said earlier that your subconscious mind governs your involuntary activities. It refers not only to things like your heart rate and breathing but also to your attitudes and behaviors. And according to the implicit convictions you have about yourself, it regulates individual attitudes and behaviors.

Let me provide you with a few examples:

-Your subconscious mind will cause you to do things that make you look stupid if you have a deep subconscious belief that you are dumb.

If you have a subconscious conviction that you are doomed to below or do not deserve to be rich, your subconscious mind may cause you to mishandle money or be attracted to situations that hold you inferior.

-- Your subconscious mind can cause you to drive people away or undermine your relationships if you subconsciously feel that you are unlovable.

-- If you subconsciously believe that you are unhealthy or will experience health problems, your subconscious mind will make your immune system not function properly, and you will get sick.

Your reality is dictated by the subconscious self-image you have of yourself. So, you need to change your subconscious self-image if you're not happy with your fact today. Your reality will change accordingly once you transform these deeply seeded negative subconscious beliefs into positive ones. That is the subconscious mind's "hidden" power, and that's what we're going to address in this book.

"The biggest revolution of our century is the realization that human beings can alter the outer aspects of life by altering the inner behaviors of their minds," said William James, the founder of American psychology. He's right, except that this definition is not modern. Remember what Solomon said, "As a man thinks in his heart, so is he," some 3,000 years ago. in the bible, we learned "transformed by our minds being renewed." So this is not a new idea. It is a universal reality that has existed for thousands of years. We don't often do an excellent job of making this versatile truth work for us. In writing this book, my purpose is to help you put this universal truth to work for you so that you can turn your life into the life you want. How to express to your subconscious mind the notion of ideal health

In Johannesburg, South Africa, a Protestant minister, I knew told me the tool he used to communicate to his subconscious mind the principle of perfect health. He had lung cancer. "His handwriting technique is as follows:" I would make sure I was completely mentally and physically comfortable many times a day. By talking to it as follows, I relaxed my body,' my feet are relaxed, my ankles are relaxed, my legs are open, my abdominal muscles relaxed, my heart and lungs are loose, my head is flexible, my whole being is fully settled.' I would be in a sleepy state after about five minutes, and then I confirmed the following fact,' God's perfection is now being expressed through me. The concept of perfect health fills my subconscious mind directly. The image God has of me is ideal, and in perfect accordance with the illustrative embodiment held in God's mind, my subconscious mind recreates my body.' This minister had remarkable healing. It is a quick, effective way of conveying to your subconscious mind the concept of perfect health.

Ambition Is Important

Many people would do reasonably well in life if they only had someone to keep stirring them up all the time, recharging them, enthusing them, continually encouraging them. Still, they have no desire to do this for themselves and thus stay in mediocrity. For their motor control, they depend upon others. You recharge them like one would a car battery when you give them a good chat, lift their expectations, and ignite their determination by telling them what's possible for them. They've been working magnificently for a couple of days, and you think they're going to turn over a new chapter and keep up their excitement, but they're going to crumble all at once. Their authority is gone, and they must be recharged. They appear utterly incapable of self-locomotion. They lack initiative, self-direction. Like the bits on a checkerboard, they must be moved around. They dazed as they are aware of standing alone, with no one to lean on or provide motor power; they do not seem to know what to do.

Some many men and women seem to be very ambitious to get on but lack self-propel power. They wait for something to happen, for someone to force them into a place to advance them, a critical friend. These people slide down the line of least resistance. They'd like success very much, but they're scared of the price. The good life is too strenuous for them. There are many problems in it, and it takes also stick and hold on in the face of impossible barriers. These people go around with an indefinite idea that there is something in the world for them somewhere and that by some chance, it will come to them if they wait long enough. At the same time, they are content to be propped up and supported by others. This lack of self-reliance, this reliance on outside forces, is fatal to all growth and accomplishment. Oh. Sam L. was irritated. He told his career therapist that he never wanted to have to find a job. "J always thought that in their companies, my father or my uncle would employ me. Even after their company collapsed, I believed that I would be employed by one of them with all the conations my family had."

There was never something Sam had considered doing for himself. Things have been done for him all his life. Yet, considering his excellent education, he had nothing to rely on but himself for the first time. Sam had the entire world to face up. He was able to assess his strengths and weaknesses, the areas in which he was satisfied and those he hated, the work prospects in a variety of fields, any extra training he required to get the kind of work wanted, and most of all, to train his mind to understand that must be self-reliant, that he could not depend on anyone but,

As a rule, you don't grow to fortune, honor, and glory by mistake from the slums and obscurity by saving someone from drowning on the seashore or finding a millionaire who loves you. Know a fundamental truth: your character, your state of mind, will always be illustrated. Character is fate. The way you think, feel and believe, the moral values you have inherited in your mind, the integrity and honesty you have built there, is character. These characteristics pay dividends.

The term TGIF, "Thank goodness it's Friday," is now known as most American workers' usual attitude. We look forward to our weekend and its break from our careers and work. There is nothing wrong with this, for in our days of rest, we can all rejoice. However, ambitious and competent individuals look forward to Monday's resumption of their work just as much. Many people are dreaming about "Blue Monday." These individuals are already resigning to their "fate" and starting to shut down their lives. Then Monday comes with a certain sense of resignation: they decreed their future consciously on Sunday, and their subconscious reacted accordingly. They probably didn't even know they had prepared ahead and thus produced their "fate." If you substitute this resignation with optimistic thoughts about the job you are doing and expect its obstacles and possibilities, you will eradicate Monday morning's blues.

Positive thinking begins with knowing the subconscious strength. Take charge of your occupation. Don't let your "career-ship" be steered by your boss, peers, or someone else. Never forget that you have the internal power to conquer opposing forces that could hinder your career development. There is nothing. There is nothing as useful as the mentality of a positive, expectant mentality that always aims for the best, the brightest, the happiest, and never allows oneself to get into a gloomy, discouraged mood. Never complete a negative declaration; instantly undo it, and wonders will occur in your life. Being imaginative, the subconscious mind will then continue similarly to create the qualities you have earnestly decreed in the experience. Imagine exactly how you will deal with the problems you face each day.

Chapter 4: Mental Healing

In Ancient Times, Mental Healings;

1. Remind yourself often that in your subconscious mind, the healing power is.

2. Know that faith is like a seed planted in the soil; it develops according to its kind. Plant in your mind the idea (source), water it, and fertilize it with expectation, and it will manifest.

3. In your mind, the concept you have for a novel, new idea, or play is actual. That's why now you can believe that you have it. Believe in the reality of your concept, plan, or invention, and it will become manifest as you do.

4. Know that your silent inner awareness of wholeness, beauty, and perfection in praying for another will modify the destructive habits of the subconscious mind of the other and produce beautiful results.

5. At different shrines, the miracle healings you hear of are due to imagination and blind faith that operate on the subconscious mind, releasing the power of healing.

6. Every illness originates in the mind. Unless there is a mental pattern matching it, nothing exists on the body.

7.The symptoms of almost any disease can be caused inside you by hypnotic suggestion. It shows you the strength of your thinking.

8. There is only one healing process, and faith is that. Only one healing power exists, namely, your subconscious mind.

9. You will get results, whether the object of your faith is genuine or fake. Your subconscious mind responds to your mind's thoughts. In your mind, look at religion as a feeling, and that will be enough.

In Modern Days, Mental Healings;

1. Find out what heals you by what it is. Know that the right guidance given to your subconscious mind will heal your body and mind.

2. Create a definite plan for your subconscious mind to turn over your demands or desires.

3. Imagine the desired end and experience the truth thereof. Follow it through, and there will be definite outcomes for you.

4. Determine what faith is. Know that in your mind, belief is a thought and what you think you make.

5. Believing in illness and anything that harms or harms you is stupid. Believe in perfect health, prosperity, harmony, fortune, and guidance from Heaven.

6. Great and noble thoughts that you habitually reflect upon becoming great deeds.

7. In your life, apply the influence of prayer therapy. Choose a specific plan, concept, or mental image. Unite with that idea mentally and emotionally, and your prayer's response will be as you remain faithful to your mental attitude.

8. Always note, you can get it by faith if you want the power to heal, which implies knowledge of your conscious and subconscious mind's workings. Confidence comes with comprehension.

9. Without any scientific understanding of the powers and forces involved, blind faith means that an individual can get results in healing.

10. Learn to pray for those loved by you who may be sick. Your mind and your ideas of fitness, vitality, and perfection working in one universal subjective mind will be felt and revived in the sense of your loved one.

In Mental Healings, Practical Methods;

1. Construct a better and more abundant life, be a mental engineer, and use tried and tested techniques.

2. Your prayer is your wish. Now, imagine the fulfillment of your desire and sense the truth of it, and you will experience the joy of your answered prayer.

3. With the safe support of cognitive science, the ability to do things the easy way.

4. Through the thoughts you think in your mind's secret studio, you can create

radiant fitness, prosperity, and happiness.

5. Experiment before you show that there is always a clear answer to your conscious thought from the limitless wisdom of your subconscious mind.

6. Feel the excitement and restfulness of awaiting the absolute fulfillment of your wish. The content of things you wish for and the proof of things not seen is every mental image you have in your mind.

7. There are a thousand words worth a mental picture. The subconscious can put every image kept in the faith-backed mind to pass.

8. In prayer, stop any effort or mental manipulation. Get into a sleepy, somnolent state and lull yourself to the feeling of sleep and to know that your prayer answered.

9. Know that the grateful heart connects with the riches of the universe.

10. To confirm is to say that it is so, and you will receive a response to your prayer as you hold this attitude of mind as real, regardless of any proof to the contrary.

11. By considering God's love and glory, produces electronic waves of harmony, well-being, and peace.

12. What you decree, and feel will come to pass as real. Harmony, fitness, prosperity and abundance Decree

4.1 The Subconscious Mind Reprogramming

By now, I hope you understand the value of eliminating negative beliefs and self-images from your subconscious mind and replacing them with positive thoughts and self-images. But how are you doing that?

There are various approaches for reprogramming the subconscious mind, but what I think is the easiest and most straightforward method of reprogramming the subconscious mind is how I will share with you in this book. This method is so simple; you will tempt to think it's not going to work. But from personal experience, I can assure you that this works! And if you're in any doubt that it's going to succeed, I've got two words of advice for you to try it.

Try that for six months, and then compare life to what your life is like right now at the end of those six months. I am sure you will be a believer in the process once you do so. This technique includes developing a series of optimistic statements (using your "conscious" mind), writing down those statements on paper, and then going through a deliberate process to incorporate those statements into your subconscious mind. They replace the old negative values previously held by your subconscious mind as the subconscious mind embraces the new affirmations. And when this happens, to fit the new self-image kept by the subconscious mind, the reality will start to change. Know, the truth will eventually make the subconscious impression of yourself that you have.

Now, let's take a look at the process. Sit down with a pencil and a pad of paper and start planning the life you want, the first thing you want to do. The way you do it is by writing down a series of statements it "exactly as you want it to be" represent you and your life. All aspects of your life, your wealth, your well-being, your relationships, your charitable giving, your faith, the home you live in, the car you drive, your lifestyle, being a person who loves and gives, how much you travel, where you travel, your job, and on and on, can be included.

How many arguments do you write down? There's no magic number, but I'll say you start with a dozen or so. I suggest this number because it is a large enough number to discuss many facets of your life. Still, it is also a small enough number that you can commit the affirmations to memory reasonably quickly, which, as you can see, can prove helpful.

I don't want to try to make your comments for you, because they have to come from you. But people have difficulty getting started with this method often. So, let me send you some example statements to make your creative juices flow.

Some examples could be:

- I own a successful company.
- I fly extensively to incredible destinations.
- I live in the home of my imagination.
- I own a lovely houseboat.
- I am blessed with an incredible family.
- I have a successful and happy marriage.

- I am a caring (husband's) wife.
- I am a mother (father) of love.
- Money flows in abundance to me naturally.
- I've got more than enough cash.
- I donate generously to worthwhile causes.
- I am blessed with exceptional fitness.
- My immune system keeps me in a steady state of well-being. I love to exercise.
- I hold my ideal weight comfortably.
- I prefer to eat nutritious foods
- I have an abundance of friends.
- I am kind, caring, and loving.
- I am a faithful and devoted friend.
- I am full of love and compassion for others.
- I am profoundly loved by my friends and family.
- I bring happiness to everyone.

Those are a few examples. The trick is planning the life you want and becoming the person you want to be.

But even if the above statements are just examples, I want you to notice two important things about them. Next, they are all in the tense of the moment. In the present tense, always write your affirmations, as though you have already completed them. The subconscious mind exists only in the present tense, so the words must be in the present tense. If you want to write a novel, instead of "I will write a book next year," you might claim, "I am a bestselling author."

"Second, all of them are" positive. Negative phrases should not be used in the affirmations. Some psychologists claim that derogatory terms like "not" are not seen or heard by the subconscious mind. So if you say, "I'm not afraid," your subconscious mind can listen to it as if you were afraid of it.

"Afraid I am." So instead, say something optimistic like "I'm calm and brave." Don't worry if it takes time for your list to come up. It's all right to spend several days writing your list of affirmations and refining them. In its own right, the process of coming up with your arguments is robust since it needs you to determine what you want to look at life. It's also all right to overhaul your list from time to time. That's a positive indication that the process is working because it means that you get more clarity on precisely what you want in life. If you discover that one of your claims no longer sounds valid to you, simply delete it or revisit it. And if you're going to, add new ones. Now, after you've established your affirmation list, what are you going to do with it? It is where it gets exciting because you are now starting to integrate these statements into your subconscious mind. And here's how you're doing that.

Simply relax, clear your mind, and concentrate on the affirmations on your list twice a day. Visualize yourself as possessing these characteristics already and having completed these objectives already. See yourself doing those activities in action and being that person. When you spend time with your list, it's up to you to determine. Still, it's saying that the first thing in the morning and just before you go to sleep at night are two perfect periods because the subconscious seems to be incredibly open to new ideas during those periods. Regardless of when you do it when you revisit your affirmations, it is necessary to place yourself in a relaxed state, because relaxation opens the door to the subconscious mind. The ideas and images you concentrate on sink back into the subconscious mind when you calm your mind and relax. So, here's what you would like to do.

Find a cozy, quiet place twice a day. Whichever you want, it can be sitting down or lying down. (It may also be late at night in bed and first thing in the morning.) It might make more sense to wait up until you have your affirmations memorized, because you will probably need to read your assertions, and while sitting, that's easier to do. one should not claim negative words. Breaths until you get into a relaxed position. Focus really on long, deep exhales. Relax every muscle in your body consciously with each exhale. Enable your body to go very limp. Spend a few seconds after taking your last deep breath to concentrate on calming the muscles in your body. If you feel entirely comfortable, start to recite your affirmations. You can say them out loud, or in your mind, you can simply say them quietly. With your eyes open, you can read them or shut your eyes and recite them from memory.

You also want to imagine each affirmation as being already real as you recite each pledge. Build a visual picture of yourself in your mind as possessing these characteristics already and possessing accomplished these goals. For the progress of the process, this visualization is essential. Your subconscious mind knows nothing right from what is imagined. The items you imagine will be recognized as actual, so let your imagination run wild as you suspect your affirmations. To feel it, you can also expand on each pledge wording and add as much detail as appropriate.

You want an emotional reaction to evoke the affirmation. It is not enough to say that you would like to experience it! The subconscious is your mind's emotional component, so you need to use emotion when programming your subconscious mind. For instance, if your written statement is "I live in my dream home," feel free to add more specifics as you recite it, and say something like, "I live overlooking the ocean in my dream home." It gives me pleasure to sit on my balcony and watch the wave collapse on the shore and smell the ocean air. And create a mental image when you speak these words. See you sitting on your dream home's balcony overlooking the ocean and watching the waves roll in and the ocean air scent. Let's look at a particular case. Suppose you have a written statement that says, "I am running a marathon successfully." As you recite it, you might add some detail and say something like, "I feel exhilarated as I reach the marathon finish line." For this achievement, my friends and family are there cheering me on. And when you recite the words, imagine yourself crossing the finish line with your hands raised in the air and cheering for you with your friends and family standing there. Feel the rush and the sense of achievement. You supercharge your assertion by adding visualization, detail, and emotion to your report. The speed and potency at which the subconscious mind embodies the affirmation are significantly enhanced. Take a deep breath, open your eyes, and go about your business after you have completed running through your promises. (Or if it's bedtime after you conduct your analysis of your affirmations, you can simply drift off to sleep.) There is no fixed period to spend each time you do this process.

Often, in just a couple of minutes, you do it fast, and sometimes you get deeply involved in the process and spend a few minutes or maybe half an hour on it. It depends on you. Let yourself in the habit of doing this a few times a day. Just like brushing your teeth and eating your meals, make it a part of your everyday routine. Every day, it becomes something that you do. Due to the theory of repetition, this is important. It is crucial to repeat the conditioning frequently while programming the subconscious mind until it embraces the new belief. You must stick with the method until the subconscious mind embraces your affirmations fully. That's because two conflicting views should not be maintained at the same time by the subconscious mind. Your subconscious mind, for instance, would either assume you are intelligent, or you are unintelligent. It's not going to consider both. So, if you're past programming has implanted the belief that you are foolish, once you override that belief and plant your subconscious mind with the idea that you are intelligent, that's what your subconscious mind would believe. If the subconscious mind embraces the new view, it will begin behaving according to the new belief.

Any unexplained changes can begin to take place in your life once you start the process of reprogramming your subconscious mind. Sometimes these alterations happen rapidly and suddenly, but sometimes they happen slowly and steadily. They happen so naturally and steadily at times that you won't even recognize them as they happen. But rest assured that the alterations are happening. Here are the kinds of improvements you can expect to see, you will gain more confidence, you will begin to believe that you can achieve your goals; you will start to see yourself, and you will start to take the required action steps to achieve your goals. Keep a good outlook, even though the outcomes do not seem to happen as quickly as you want them to. It is also necessary to "anticipate" the changes in your life that will arise. Expectation, when you give your subconscious mind instructions, is a self-fulfilling prophecy. When the subconscious mind anticipates something, it makes the thing happen. As your subconscious mind embraces these new values, it is also essential to take "conscious" steps towards your objectives. For example, I used the bar earlier that "I ran a marathon successfully" might be one of your affirmations. In this example, you take the necessary steps to train for a marathon while you embed this affirmation into your subconscious mind. In your city, you can begin researching marathon races and decide which one you want to run. You will set up a training schedule and a timetable to move you towards this target. So, as you pursue this phase of incorporating these new beliefs in your subconscious mind, ask yourself regularly what steps you can take to shift yourself in the direction of your objectives on a conscious basis. You will find a renewed faith when you do this to attain and achieve every one of your affirmations. For six months, commit to this phase, then look at the changes in your life that have occurred. I think you'll understand the strength of this method once you do this.

4.2 Reprogram your Subconscious Mind with Technology

I have outlined what I think is one of the easiest, most straightforward, and most effective ways to reprogram your subconscious mind and construct the life you want. I genuinely believe that you will successfully change your subconscious mind's deep-seated values and create the life you crave if you follow the method outlined in the previous chapter. You watch a short video a few times a day on your computer, your iPad, your mobile phone, or some other similar gadget, instead of going through the twice-daily routine of concentrating on your statements.

The app is called Mind Movies, and it takes the optimistic claims and blends those claims with the images and music you pick. A short video or movie personalized to represent the life of your dreams is the result. You watch your Mind Movie a few times a day, and these affirmations and images are soaked up by your subconscious mind and go to work reprogramming your subconscious mind. Note, as I have said many times in this book, eventually, your truth will fit the subconscious picture you have of yourself. You are also setting the groundwork for building the life you want by using your Mind Movie to boost your subconscious self-image. In addition to the method outlined in the previous chapter, some people prefer to use Mind Movies, while others use Mind Movies as their only tool for reprogramming their subconscious mind. I used Mind Movies extensively on my own, and without reservation, I can tell you that it is ultimately one of the most useful resources I have ever used. And it's straightforward to use technology. You can make your very own personal Mind Movie if you can use a mouse and a keyboard. It is also very cheap, making it within practically anyone's grasp. I built a particular page on my website where I posted a Mind Movie sample, I made for you and details how you can make your Mind Movie if you want to know more about Mind Movies. If you're reading this eBook on a computer that allows you to watch videos, you can simply visit the page and watch the video by clicking the link below. Otherwise, to protect the connection, you can type it into your computer or another video-capable device.

4.3 The Function of Prayer in Your Subconscious Mind's Reprogramming

This part gears toward faith. If you're not a person of faith, I hope this chapter will not put you off. In reprogramming your subconscious mind, the other techniques we've explored in this book will also work for you. But if like I am, you are a person of faith, I want to share with you how your life of prayer can overload your efforts to program your subconscious mind. Importantly I want to make that your efforts to reprogram your subconscious mind will help your life of worship (making it more efficient). Your experience of prayer will support your efforts to reprogram your subconscious mind. To benefit each other, they work hand in hand to help you make the improvements you want. William James, the founder of American psychology, emphasized that any image kept in mind and assisted by faith brings to pass by the subconscious mind.

For good prayer, faith widely recognizes as essential. And your confidence, if it instills in your conscious mind, is not complete. Trust must also be ingrained in your subconscious mind to be successful. Jesus insisted on an attitude of faith, and he often bound the recipients' religion or belief to his divine works. "That's why we hear Jesus saying stuff " It happens to you according to your faith "and" According to your faith,

"For one who believes, anything is possible."

Jesus also said, "In prayer, whatever you ask for, believe that you have earned it, and it will be yours."

Note the order of what he is saying,

Phase1 to "ask" is.

Phase 2 is to "believe it has been earned by you already."

Phase 3 is: "It's going to be yours."

Note that, long before it is physically present in our lives, we instruct to assume that we have already earned it. The true expression of faith is this. For specific individuals, that are a stretch, but let me give you an example to help make it more understandable. Just imagine I'm giving you $10,000 for a moment, but instead of handing you $10,000 in cash, I'm placing it in your name on a certificate of deposit. That money is yours, but until the certificate of deposit matures, you cannot withdraw it and hold it in your hands. That's the way I like to look at this whole notion of believing that, long before it is physically present in our lives, we have earned something. When I ask in prayer for something, I try to think of it in my account as being on deposit. It's mine now, and before I physically obtain it, I just need to wait until the maturity date. The maturity date comes easily sometimes, and other times it takes a while. But I need to keep believing that even though I'm waiting to receive it physically, it's already mine. Your efforts to reprogram your subconscious mind will help (make it more effective) your prayer life, as I said earlier, and in turn, your prayer life will support your efforts to reprogram your subconscious mind. One at a time, let's look at these definitions. Let's look first at how your attempts to reprogram your subconscious mind help your life of prayer.

I stressed the importance of using the present tense in this book, seeing yourself as having already accomplished what you want or have already been the person you wish to be. You are enhancing the trust or conviction that you have already earned what you want by using the present tense while you program your subconscious mind. For good prayer, this faith or sentence is what is required. As Jesus said, you must first believe that you have already earned it, and then it will be yours. You deepen your faith and your values by implanting these values in your subconscious mind, which, in turn, increases the efficacy of your prayers.

From the other side of the coin, let's look at it now. In your attempt to reprogram your subconscious mind, let's look at how your prayer life helps you. If you have faith in a Higher Force whom you believe hears your prayers and wishes to answer your prayers by what is best for you, then your prayers will be highly successful in implanting your subconscious mind with optimistic values and hopes. The very act of worship involves the subconscious mind, especially the deep prayer in which you remain and concentrate intently. It profoundly influences the values present in your subconscious mind when you combine the act of worship with a sincere conviction that your prayers are being heard and answered. So your life of prayer will help you reprogram your subconscious mind successfully. And how do you work alongside your other attempts to reprogram your subconscious mind in the course of organizing your prayer life?

We have previously explored developing a series of optimistic affirmations for the life you want or the things you want in life. So, here's how to integrate it into your life of prayer. Start by praying an earnest prayer when you come up with the list, asking for each of those things to be valid in your life, and stating that you have faith that these things are yours. Your subsequent prayers regularly should be prayers of thanksgiving after you have prayed that initial prayer asking for these things, that you have received the items you asked for (or are in the process of obtaining those, if that sounds more fitting to you.)

So, some examples of these thanksgiving prayers may be:

Thank you for the excellent company you brought me. Thank you for making me healthier and happier every day. Thank you for my life of caring relationships. Thank you for the happiness that I feel every day. With outstanding fitness, thank you for blessing me. With a lovely and wonderful home, thank you for blessing me. Thank you for giving me a marriage that is happy and successful. You're getting the idea. Only express appreciation and gratitude for having received or accomplished your goals and affirmations already.

I like to include with each affirmation a message of gratitude. For example, if my assertion is, "I finish a marathon effectively," I will state the claim and imagine myself crossing the finish line to the cheers of my family and friends. And then I'm going to add a short thanksgiving sentence, such as "Thank you, God, for allowing me to complete this marathon." I do this for each of my affirmations, and I have found it a compelling approach. Regularly, put this into effect. I don't mean a week or two of trying it out. On an ongoing basis, I mean, put it into effect, and watch the changes taking place in your life. You'll be amazed, I think.

4.4 Fear conquering

Fear and anxiety draw us to the very things we fear. The habit of fear impairs health, shortens life, and paralyzes productivity. Doubt and fear indicate failure; trust, fear, is an optimist. Confidence is the ultimate cure, for certainty sees the silver lining, the light behind the cloud, while fear sees only darkness and shadows. Fear is looking down and anticipating the worst; trust is looking up and expects the best. Fear is pessimistic; there is optimism in faith. Fear still forecasts failure; confidence forecasts achievement. Delete all false assumptions, prejudices, and superstitions from your thought. Order your mind and emotions to truly recognize that what you are looking for already exists in the Infinite Mind, and all you have to do is to mentally and emotionally locate it. Too many people will be afraid to use their minds. They let their minds according to the views of their superiors or strong-minded colleagues on the job. Don't allow it to happen to you.

Build up your subconscious mind's capacity to resist others' dominance and assert your right to influence your destiny. You're so much better than any material error that may happen to you. You are superior to them, no matter what reverses, what disappointments or failures, you come to you. Don't ever lose equanimity.

4.5 Honoring Your Originality

There are several ways in which one can generate imagination. Start by exploring current techniques, then ask yourself how they can be made better and use your imagination to find ways to do it. Here are some specific ways to hone your artistic abilities. Everyone should be imaginative. To be an innovator, you don't need to be Edison or Bill Gates. The ability to stretch your imagination is within you. To grow it, it is up to you. You have power over any situation or condition by your ability to visualize the result. Shape a mental image of its fulfillment in your mind if you want to bring about the realization of some wish, wish, concept, or plan. Imagine, always, the truth of your wish. It will infiltrate your subconscious mind in this way, and you will force it into existence. Any concept or desire can be clothed and objectified in your imagination. You can imagine abundance where scarcity is, efficacy where inefficiency is, and development hampered by stagnation. When faced with related situations, observe what other businesses have done. You may be able to deal with the issue effectively by incorporating methods that have worked for them. Use your faculties of imagination. Find areas that could strengthen your job or your business. Don't be afraid to try new ways. You may have setbacks, but you can succeed in all of your endeavors by honing your creative powers.

Chapter 5: The Subconscious Mind Is A Success Partner

Success implies living efficiently. On this plane, a long period of harmony, joy, and happiness may be termed progress. The eternal experience of these virtues is the everlasting life of which Jesus speaks. Real things in life are intangible, such as prosperity, harmony, honesty, comfort, and happiness. They come from Man's Deep Self. In our subconscious, meditating on these virtues creates these treasures of heaven. There is no consumption of moth and rust, and where thieves do not break through and steal.

The Three Performance Steps

Let's talk about three steps to success: finding out what you love to do is the first step to win and then do it. Success is in enjoying your work. And if a man is a psychiatrist, getting a certificate and sticking it on the wall is not sufficient for him; he must keep up with the times, attend conferences, and research the mind and its operations. The prolific psychiatrist visits clinics and reads the latest scientific papers. In other words, he tells about the most sophisticated ways to relieve human misery. The psychiatrist or doctor who is successful must have the interest of his patients at heart.

Someone might say, "How can I put into operation the first step?" In such a situation, pray for guidance as follows: "My subconscious mind's infinite wisdom shows my true place in life to me." Repeat this prayer to your deeper mind softly, positively, and lovingly. The answer will come to you as a feeling, a hunch, or a tendency in a specific direction as you persist with faith and trust. It will come only and gently to you, and as a quiet inner consciousness.

The second step to success is to specialize and know more about it than anyone else in some specific work branch. If a young man chooses chemistry as his occupation, he should focus on one of this area's many components. He ought to give his chosen specialty all of his time and attention. He should be sufficiently excited to try to know anything about his profession that is available; he should know more than anyone else if possible. A young man should be keenly interested in his work and willing to serve the world. May the one who is greatest among you become your servant. In this attitude of mind, there is an excellent contrast to a man who wishes to make a living ." "Getting by" is not a real achievement.

The motivation of man must be more robust, more honorable, and more altruistic. He must serve others, casting his bread on the waters in this way.

The most significant one is the third stage. You must be sure that not only redounds to your success the thing you want to do. Your desire must not be egoistic; humanity must benefit from it. It is necessary to form the direction of a complete circuit. In other words, with the purpose of blessing or serving the earth, your idea must move forward. Then it will come back to you, pushed down, shaken together, and overflowing. The loop or full circuit does not create if it is to help you solely, and you may encounter a short course in your life that may consist of restriction or illness.

5.1 Your Subconscious Mind and Joy

William James said that the most astonishing revelation of the 19th century was the influence of a faith-touched subconscious mind. Inside you, there is immense strength. As you develop a sublime faith in this force, happiness will come to you. You'll make your dreams come true, then. Through the beautiful power of your subconscious mind, you will emerge victorious over any loss and understand the cherished desires of your heart. It is the sense of the joyful one who trusts in the Lord [spiritual laws of the subconscious mind]. It would be best if you chose happiness. A habit is a joy.

Whatever stuff is real, think about it. When you open your eyes, tell yourself, today, I choose happiness at the start of the day. Today, I shall determine success. Today, I decided on the right action. Today, I will choose love and goodwill for all. I want to peace today. Through this affirmation, pour life, love, and interest, and you have chosen happiness.

Several times a day, give thanks for all your blessings. Also, pray for the peace, happiness, and prosperity of all your family members, your friends, and all individuals everywhere. You must sincerely desire to be happy. Without desire, nothing does. With wings of imagination and confidence, passion is a wish. Imagine your desire's fulfillment, and feel its truth, and it will come to pass. In the answered prayer, happiness comes. You will become very depressed and unhappy by continuously dwelling on thoughts of fear, worry, rage, hate, and failure. Know what your thoughts make of it is your life. You cannot buy happiness with all the money in the world. Some millionaires are very happy, and some are very sad. Some people are pleased, and others are unfortunate.

Some people are happy on their own, and some are very sad. The kingdom of joy is in your thoughts and emotions. Happiness is a peaceful mind's harvest. Anchor your thoughts on peace, equilibrium, safety, and divine guidance, and joy will be productive in your mind. The block to your happiness is not there. External things are not causative; they are consequences, not causes. From the only artistic principle inside you, take your cue. Your thinking is the cause, and a new reason has a unique effect.

Seek happiness, which brings forth the supreme and the best in him, is the happiest man. God is inside, is the greatest and the strongest in him.

5.2 Your Unconscious Mind and Human Harmonious Ties

A recording machine is your subconscious mind, which reproduces your normal thought. Think good of each other, and you feel good of yourself. A feeling that is hateful or resentful is a mental poison. To think I'll of yourself is not to think I'll of another for doing so. In your world, you're the only thinker, and your ideas are imaginative. Your mind is a creative medium; thus, you bring to pass through your own experience, what you think and feel about each other. It is the Golden Rule's psychological meaning. Just as you'd like a man to think about you, think about them in the same way. To cheat, rob, or defraud another brings to yourself lack, loss, and limitation. Your subconscious mind documents your inner motives, thoughts, and emotions. These are negative; in countless ways, loss, regulation, and distress come to you. The good that you do, the kindness that you offer, the love and interest that you send forth, in many ways, all will come back to you. In your world, you're the only thinker. You are accountable for the way you think about each other. The other person is not responsible for your feelings about him, remember. They reproduce your thoughts. What do you think of the other man now? Become emotionally mature and allow other individuals to differ from you. Their right to disagree with you is fair, and you have the same ability to disagree with them. Without being disagreeable, you should disagree. The animals pick up the vibrations of your anxiety and bite at you.

They will never attack you if you love animals. Many undisciplined human beings are just as sensitive as dogs, cats, and other species. Your inner voice, reflecting your silent thoughts and feelings, is experienced in others' reactions towards you. Wish the other person what you wish for yourself. The secret to harmonious human relationships is this. Change your idea and your employer's estimate. He follows the Golden Rule and the Law of Love, feeling, and knowing, and he will respond accordingly. The other person is unable to annoy you or irritate you unless you allow him to. You are imaginative in your thinking; you will bless him. If someone calls you a skunk, you have the freedom to say to another, "Your soul fills with God's peace." Love is the answer to all questions. Love is understanding, goodwill, and honoring one another's divinity. You wouldn't hate a disabled person or a hunchback. You'd have sympathy. Have compassion and empathy for negatively conditioned emotional hunchbacks. To understand all is to forgive all. Rejoice in one another's success, promotion, and good fortune. You attract good luck from yourself by doing so. Never surrender to others' dramatic scenes

and tantrums. Appeasement is never victorious. Oh, don't be a doormat. A good will what's right. Please stick to your ideal, understanding that Riga disabled person and real are the mental outlooks that give you harmony, satisfaction, and joy. What blesses you, everything blesses you. Love is everything you owe to every person globally, and love wishes everyone what you want for yourself, luck, happiness, and all life's blessings.

5.3 How to Forever Remain Young in Spirit

Your subconscious mind is never aging. It's eternal, ageless, and limitless. It is a part of God's infinite reason that has never been born and will never die. Any spiritual quality or power cannot predicate on fatigue or old age. The virtues and values that never grow old are patience, compassion, truthfulness, modesty goodwill, goodwill, harmony, and brotherly love. Here on this plane of life, if you continue to produce these qualities, you will remain young in spirit.

Some years ago, I recalled reading an article in one of our magazines saying that a group of distinguished medical men at the De Courcy Clinic in Cincinnati, Ohio, claimed that years alone were not responsible for causing degenerative disorders. These same doctors claimed that it is the fear of time that has a detrimental aging effect on our minds and bodies, not time itself and that the neurotic fear of the consequences of time may well be the cause of premature aging. Over the years of my public life, I have had the opportunity to research the biographies of the prominent men and women who have continued their productive activities into the years well beyond the usual span of life.

In old age, some of them attain their excellence. It was my high to meet and know countless people of no prominence who belonged to those hardy mortals in their lesser domain who have shown that the old age of itself does not kill the mind and body's creative forces.

He had grown old in his life of thinking; I called an old acquaintance in London, England, a couple of years ago. He was very ill and gave in to his years of progression. Our conversation exposed his physical weakness, sense of anger, and an almost lifelessness approaching general deterioration. He screamed out that he was worthless, and nobody wanted him. He betrayed his false philosophy with an expression of hopelessness: "We are born, we grow up, we grow old, we are good for nothing, and that's the end."

The chief reason for his sickness was this mental attitude of futility and worthlessness. He only looked forward to senescence and nothing after that. Indeed, in his thinking life, he had grown old, and his subconscious mind brought about all the evidence of his usual thinking.

The dawn of wisdom is the age. Sadly, many individuals have the same mindset as this unhappy man. They are frightened of what they call "old age," the end, and extinction, which means they are terrified of life. Yet, life is eternal. Age is not the flight of years but wisdom's dawn. Learning is an understanding of the subconscious mind's immense spiritual powers and the knowledge of how to apply these powers to lead a complete and happy life. Once, get it out of your head that 65, 75, or 85 years of age is synonymous with the end for you. It can be the beginning, better than you have ever experienced, of a glorious, fruitful, active, and most beneficial life pattern. Believe this, expect it, and your subconscious will bring it on.

5.4 Welcome the progress

Old age is no tragic event. What we call the phase of aging is truly a transition. As every stage of human life is a step forward on a journey that has no end, it is to be accepted joyfully and gladly. Man has powers that transcend his corporeal powers. He's got senses that go beyond his five physical senses. Today, scientists find that something aware in man can leave his present body and travel thousands of miles to see, hear, touch, and talk to people, even though his physical body never goes the couch on which it rests. The life of man is divine and everlasting. He never needs to grow old because Life, or God, cannot grow old. God is life, the Bible says. Life is eternal, indestructible, self-renewing, and is the reality of all men.

Survival Proof

The data obtained by both Great Britain and America's psychological research societies are compelling. Based on distinguished scientists' results on survival after so-called death, you can go to any sizeable metropolitan library and get volumes on The Proceedings of the Psychical Research Society. In the Case for Psychic Survival by Hereward Carrington, Director of the American Psychical Institute, you will find a startling report on scientific experiments establishing the reality of life after death.

"Thomas Edison, the electrical wizard, was asked by a woman," Mr. What's electricity, Edison? "He responded," Madame, that's electricity. Use it.' Electricity is a name that we give a supernatural force that we do not entirely understand, but about the concept of electricity and its uses, we learn what we can. In countless ways, we use it. The scientist, through his eyes, is unable to see an electron. Still, he acknowledges it as a scientific fact because it is the only factual finding that suits his other experimental proof. Existence, we can't see. We know we're alive, however. Life is, and we are here in all its beauty and glory to express it.

Spirit and mind do not grow old.

The Bible states, and this is everlasting life that the only true God should know you. The man who thinks or believes that all there is to life is the earthly cycle of birth, puberty, youth, maturity, and old age, must indeed be pitied. Such a man has no anchor, no dream, no vision, and to him, life has no purpose. This kind of conviction leads to anger, stagnation, cynicism, and a feeling of hopelessness that leads to all types of neurosis and mental aberrations. If you can't play a quick tennis game or swim as fast as your son, or if your body has slowed down, or if you're strolling, remember that life is always a new kind of clothing. What do men call death is only a journey into another dimension of life to a new city? I tell men and women that they should gracefully embrace what we reach old age in my lectures. A generation has its glory, its elegance, the wisdom that belongs to it. The qualities that never grow old or die are peace, love, joy, beauty, happiness, knowledge, goodwill, and understanding. A poet and philosopher, Ralph Waldo Emerson, said, "We do not count the years of a man until he has nothing else to count." Your character, mind's quality, faith, and convictions are not subject to decay.

You're as young as you thought.

"Every few years, I give public lectures at Caxton Hall, London, England, and after one of these lectures, a surgeon told me," I am 84 years of age. "I work every morning, visit patients in the afternoons, and write in the evening for medical and other scientific journals." His mentality was that he was as helpful as he felt was and that he was as young as his feelings. "He said to me, "What you said is real, 'Man is as powerful as he thinks is and as precious as thinks he is.' This surgeon has not capitulated to years of advancement. He believes that he is invincible. If I were to pass on tomorrow, I'd be operating on people in the next dimension, not with the scalpel of a surgeon, but with mental and spiritual surgery, "was his final statement to me."

Your grey hair is an asset to you!

Don't ever leave a job and say, "I'm retired; I'm old; I'm done." That would be death, stagnation, and you'd be done.

Some men are 30 years of age, while others are 80 years of age. The mind is the master weaver, the architect, the sculptor, and the designer George George. At 90, Bernard Shaw was active, and he had not relaxed the artistic quality of his mind from active duty. I meet men and women who tell me that when they say they are over 40, some employers almost shut the door in their faces. On the part of employers, this attitude should be considered cold, callous, evil, and utterly void of compassion and understanding. The total focus tends to be on youth, i.e., to earn recognition; you must be under 35 years of age. Indeed, the logic behind this is very superficial. He would know that the man or woman was not selling his age or grey hair if the employer stopped and realized, instead, he was willing to offer his skills, his knowledge, and his expertise gathered from years of experience in the marketplace of life.

5.5 Age Is an Advantage

Your age should be a distinct advantage for every organization because of experience and implementation over the years of the Golden Rule ideals and the law of love and goodwill. Your grey hair should have more incredible knowledge, abilities, and understanding if you have any. To any organization, your emotional and spiritual maturity should be a tremendous blessing. When he is 65 years of age, a man did not ask to resign. It is the time of life when, based on his experience and insight into the company's nature, he could be most useful in handling staff problems, making plans for the future, making decisions, and guiding others in the field of creative ideas.

In Hollywood, a motion-picture writer told me he had to write scripts that would appeal to the twelve-year-old mind. If the great masses of individuals expect to become emotionally and spiritually mature, this is a sad state of affairs. It implies that, even though youth stands for inexperience, lack of discernment, and hasty judgment, it emphasizes a child.

Keep the Best

I am now thinking of a 65-year-old man who is frantically trying to stay young. Every Sunday, he swims with young men, goes on long hikes, plays tennis, and praises his prowess and his physical abilities, saying, "Look, I can keep up with the best of them!" The great truth should be remembered: as a man thinks in his heart, so is he. Diets, activities, and games of all kinds are not going to keep this guy young. He must observe that he, under his thinking processes, grows old or remains young. Via your emotions, your subconscious mind is conditioned. If your thoughts are continually on the beautiful, the noble, and the good, you will remain youthful regardless of the chronological years.

Old Age Fear

Work said that things that I feared incredibly came upon me. Many individuals fear old age and are uncertain about the future because, as the years advance, they anticipate mental and physical deterioration. What they feel and think to pass. As you lose interest in life, as you cease to dream, hunger for new truths, and discover new worlds to conquer, you grow old. You will be young and vital when your mind is open to fresh thoughts, unique desires, and when you lift the curtain and let in the sunlight and inspiration of the new truths of life and the universe.

You've got a lot to give

Realize that you have a lot to offer, whether you are 65 or 95 years of age. You may help stabilize, advise, and guide the younger generation. You can benefit from your experience, your knowledge, and your wisdom. It would help if you still looked forward to seeing eternal life at all times. You will find that the glories and wonders of life you will never cease to unveil. Every moment of the day try to learn something new, and you will find your mind will always be young. One hundred and ten years old While lecturing in Bombay, India, I was introduced to a guy who said he was 110 years old some years ago. He had the gorgeous face that I've ever seen. He seemed trans-figured by the radiance of the light within himself. In his eyes, there was a remarkable elegance that suggested he had grown old with pleasure in years and without any hint had dimmed its lights.

Retirement Is A New Undertaking

Be sure your mind never withdraws. It has to be like a parachute which, until it opens up, is no good. Be open to new ideas and be receptive. I saw men aged 65 and 70 retires. They appeared to rot away, and they passed away in a matter of months. They felt life was at an end.

A new venture, a unique opportunity, a new direction, the beginning of the fulfillment of a long dream, maybe seems like retirement. Hearing a man say, "What am I going to do now that I am retired?" is inexpressibly sad. "He says, in essence," I am dead physically and mentally. "My mind is bankrupt with ideas." All of this is a false image. The simple truth is that you will do more at 90 than you did at 60, and through your new studies and interests, you grow in experience and comprehension of life and the world every day. He graduated and got a better job. A few months ago, a manager living near me was forced to retire because he had reached the age of 65. He said to me, " I look upon my retirement as a promotion from kindergarten to the first grade. "He philosophized in this manner: He said, went up the ladder when he left high school by going to college. It was a step forward in his education and understanding of life in general, he realized. Similarly, he said, he was now free to do the things he had always wanted to do, and so his retirement was just another step up the ladder of life and wisdom.

He came to the wise conclusion that he was no longer going to concentrate on making a living. He was now going to pay all of his attention to living life. He is an amateur photographer, and he has taken further courses on this subject. He went on a world tour and made films of famous locations. He now lectures before numerous parties, lodges, and societies and is in high demand. There are endless ways of taking an interest in something outside of you that is worthwhile. Get excited about new creative ideas, make spiritual progress, and keep learning and growing. In this manner, you remain young in heart, for you are hungering and thirsting for new realities, and your body will represent your thoughts at all times. You have to be a producer rather than a prisoner of society. The newspapers are aware that the elderly's voting population of the elderly is increasing by leaps and bounds in the California elections. It means hear them in the state legislature and the halls of Congress as well. I assume a federal law would enforce banning employers from discrimination on the grounds of age against men and women. A 65-year-old man may be psychologically, physically, and physiologically younger than many men at 30. It is stupid and ridiculous to tell a man he cannot hires because he is over 40. It's like telling him that the scrap heap or the junk pile is ready for him.

5.8 Youth's Secret

To recapture the days of your childhood, sense your subconscious mind's miraculous, healing, self-renewing force flowing through your entire being. Know and feel that you are inspired, lifted, rejuvenated, revitalized, and recharged spiritually. As in the days of your youth, you can bubble over with enthusiasm and joy, for the simple reason that you can always male-tally and emotionally recapture the joyful state.

The candle that shines upon your head is divine intelligence, and it reveals to you all that you need to know; it allows you, regardless of appearance, to affirm the presence of your goodness. You walk by your subconscious mind's guidance, for you see the dawn is coming, and the shadows are fleeing away.

5.9 Get a vision

Instead of saying, "I am old," say, "I am wise in the Divine Lifeway." Refuse to be hypnotized by the propaganda of this sort. Claim life and not death. As happy, radiant, prosperous, serene, and healthy, get a vision of you.

Conclusion

I hope you have enjoyed this excellent book. When you take to heart the lessons found in this book and integrate them into your life,

your dream life will create. You are here to lead a happy life, a life full of love, peace, happiness, and a life whole of richness. Start releasing the riches of the treasure house within you now. Where your vision lies, you go.